Honor Your Father and Your Mother

Reflections on the Commandments

Paul Tammi

ST. PAUL BOOKS & MEDIA

Nihil Obstat:
   Very Rev. Timothy J. Shea, VF

Imprimatur:
   Bernard Cardinal Law

February 3, 1995

The Scripture quotations contained herein are from the *Revised Standard Version Bible with the Apocrypha/Deuterocanonical Books*, copyrighted © 1973 by the Division of Christian Education of the National Council of Churches of Christ in the U.S.A., and are used by permission. All rights reserved.

Excerpt from *Letters and Papers from Prison* by Dietrich Bonhoeffer, copyright © 1953, 1967, 1971 by SCM Press, Ltd. Used by permission of Macmillan Publishing Company.

Photo credits: FSP 8; Mimi Forsyth 16, 36; SEA 22; Mary Emmanuel Alves, FSP 28, 57; CLEO 47; Christine Noell 54
Design by Mary Joseph Peterson, FSP

ISBN: 0-8198-3374-6

Original title: *Onora il padre e la madre*

Copyright © 1991, Figlie di San Paolo, Milan, Italy

Translated from the Italian by Mary James Berger, FSP

English edition copyright © 1995, Daughters of St. Paul

Printed and published in the U.S.A. by Pauline Books & Media, 50 St. Paul's Avenue, Boston, MA 02130.

Pauline Books & Media is the publishing house of the Daughters of St. Paul, an international congregation of women religious serving the Church with the communications media.

1 2 3 4 5   99 98 97 96 95

CONTENTS

Introduction 4

Overview of *Honor Your Father and Your Mother* 6

Who Are My Father and My Mother? 9

Views—The "Father" and Fathers 14

A Communion to be Created 17

Views—We Belong to One Another Forever 24

Views—It's Wonderful to Drink from this Pitcher! 26

A Communion to Multiply 29

Views—Can't We Build Bridges? 34

Aren't Two Parents Enough? 37

Views—The Child of...Several Parents 43

Honor Until the Expiration Date? 45

Views—What Else Can the Fourth Commandment
  Mean Today? 51

Views—Roots 53

Let's Celebrate the Lord Our God 56

Witness—Mary Is Our Mother 58

Notes 60

About the Author 61

About this Series 61

INTRODUCTION

No reader over forty can forget how much the fourth commandment, "Honor your father and your mother," was emphasized in catechetical instruction and in the moral counsel given in confession.

Many may also recall the feelings of guilt, anger, frustration and discouragement which sprang from a difficult relationship with their father or mother.

Today, due to cultural changes, the relations between children and parents have changed and require, especially of those who do pastoral work, a sensitivity definitely different from the somewhat "categorical" attitude of the past. But has the commandment become less important?

Those who don't go along with the current opinion—that is, that the Ten Commandments are now worthless or should have been abolished or replaced by "other commandments," even in the daily examination of conscience—can't help but feel an urgent need to restore the fourth commandment to the place it deserves.

There are many reasons for this urgency, among which are: the increased difficulty in establishing motivation and time for communication between parents and children; the undoubted "rediscovery" on the part of young people that the family is a place not only for shelter and living quarters, but also for that sincere search for human warmth which is found less and less in the traditional gathering places for young people. Another factor is that almost all the imbalances during adolescence have their origin in a difficult relationship with parents.

On this last point there are no doubts. Those who spend all or part of their lives helping young people are familiar with the subtle and often corrosive drama that arises—around the age of thirteen or fourteen—between them and the rest of the family. And if we see young teens depressed, sulking, tense, distracted, it's very likely that the first acts of the drama have already begun in their lives.

This booklet is intended to help the reader interpret the fourth commandment as an unending call to create in the family the bases for harmonious living together, for communication that is liberating, for a peaceful existence in the sense of the Gospel, one which is not free from the daily burdens and crosses, but which is lived in maturity and in the firmness of the Christian faith.

This call is for everyone. We are all children and we are all destined by God for some form of fatherhood or motherhood. There is no valid affection that does not model itself on the self-giving love of God for each individual person.

Overview

Honor Your Father and Your Mother

This booklet is divided into five parts or units, as an aid to perceiving step by step the motivations and profound relevance of the fourth commandment.

Beginning from the incontestable fact that each person has come into the world without personally willing to do so, we face the fundamental question: "Where do I come from? Whom do I come from?" It is a matter of discovering the origin of our own existence and of our own personality. Believers are led to understand that our primary origin is God himself, and that man and woman become his instruments in time and space.

The natural human community that is created then develops and grows, continually giving life—understood as vitality, energy, and the possibility for the maturation and development of the whole person. Herein lies the need for a plan for growth, based on some fundamental values.

"Honor your father and your mother" is, in a certain sense, the synthesis of these values. Even today the commandment points to the family's need to follow guidelines and develop a specific direction, which naturally the parents should offer and have respected. But "honor one another" also becomes the means for providing everyone with that peace and harmony in which each matures the awareness of personal freedom, which is a gift of God and a fundamental right of the person.

The five units are:

Who Are My Father and My Mother?

A Communion to be Created

A Communion to Multiply

Aren't Two Parents Enough?

Honor Until the Expiration Date?

Each unit is developed in three parts:

Reading Life
We begin from the analysis of human experience.

Listening to the Word
We listen to and seek to understand the plan of God.

If You Wish to Grow
Questions and thoughts are offered to stimulate personal and group reflection.

The Views sections that complete each unit offer another link to the reality of daily life.

Who Are My Father and My Mother?

Reading Life

"Your children are not your children. They are the sons and daughters of life's longing for itself.... You are the bows from which your children as living arrows are shot forth."[1]

This is how The Prophet of Kahlil Gibran speaks to parents. We become children—he says—because life needs children. Life generates life and is reproduced in each child that, at every moment, comes into this world. Life itself needs children.

Have you ever noticed the reality which everyone now calls "affective needs"? Did you ever reflect on the fact that a number of your excesses, problems and attitudes may depend on the need you have for affection, for greater affection?

When you feel this need, you are rediscovering the strong bond that unites you to life. So if life needs you, its child, you have an even greater need for life, your mother. You therefore need to be a child.

According to Eric Berne, the founder of the therapeutic method called "transactional analysis," each person living in this world "is hungry for caresses." That is, each of us needs to be touched and recognized by others. By caresses are meant "any act which implies recognition of the presence of another."

The desire for affection is especially seen in young people. Without exaggeration, it seems that the situation in which we live can be defined as "a world without a father."

Yorick Spiegel, a German theologian, writes: "On the one hand, the son and daughter find in the family a place of safety and assistance when faced with the world of social power with which they come into contact, first in educational institutions and, later, in the exercise of their profession. They are in the family, but they also face violent conflicts.... They experience above all the instability of marriage relationships."

And so, family...yes and family...no. The home can be a place of refuge, of protection from a hostile and difficult world. At the same time it is often a place in which the search for a balanced, serene and stable father/motherhood is often disappointed.

Listening to the Word

To listen means to participate with the whole person (body, mind, affection) in what is being proclaimed or proposed—even more so when the source of the proposal is what Christians call the "Word of God," that is, the Word inspired, guaranteed and accompanied by God himself.

This Word does not resolve problems directly nor does it offer immediate solutions. It is to be "listened to," that is, assimilated, digested, reread and repeated. It gradually forms our consciences.

Listening to the Word is a long task that requires perseverance. Don't get discouraged; we can succeed with God's help.

Our ancestors the Hebrews, "our older brothers," as John Paul II called them in the synagogue in Rome, have been pilgrims, strangers in many lands, but their strength has always been their fidelity to the Father.

"I will be his father, and he shall be my son" (2 Sam 7:14). With this promise made to David, we can sum up God's love for his people Israel.

Israel had many human fathers; the history of salvation calls them "patriarchs." Their great dignity, which made them credible, was the promise they had received from God: a promise of good, of strength, of prosperity, which through them was given to all the people.

We could say that the patriarchs were the living guarantee that God would continue to bless his people.

Their personal stories, rich in dramatic events, high points and low points, are recorded in the book of Genesis.

The so-called "cycle of Abraham" (Gen 12:1 to 25:11) is a series of thrilling stories. However, it isn't to be read only as a history, or as the description of events. We need to listen to it as the witness of faith of an entire people.

The name Abraham means "father of a multitude." Because of his courage, his availability, his extraordinary ability to depend on God in everything, we too are born as Christians; we too are the heirs of the blessing of Abraham.

The "cycle of Jacob," too (Gen 25:19 to 35:29), will lead you to relive the history and faith of a fragile man, one like us, tempted to corner fortune and even God's benevolence by means of deceit. Stricken and then restored by God, he recognizes his weakness and the need to be God's obedient, faithful child.

And precisely because he surrenders himself as a child and lets himself be guided by God, Jacob too becomes a father, one of the fathers of Israel.

The Old Testament does not present a theory, but a lived experience. It is the experience of a divine fatherhood, of an immense goodness, of the great tenderness of God for us who are called to submit to God in full trust.

Jesus then reveals God to us as Father.

He reveals the profoundly human face of God, since this face, this image, thenceforth for us Christians has been Jesus himself.

"Have I been with you so long, and yet you do not know me, Philip? He who has seen me has seen the Father" (Jn 14:9).

If You Wish to Grow

The need to be a child, the desire for a selfless, genuine affection without reserve, leads many young persons to ask themselves: Who are my mother and my father?

Sometimes this need for affection may clash with another need, that of autonomy, which is "the need to actively direct one's own life, to resist pressures, to avoid being a slave to domineering authorities, to be independent and free to act according to personal criteria."

Think about this series of needs. You must feel them, too. But you probably can't deny that, in order to satisfy them, you wouldn't want to renounce the affection of those whose father/motherhood is a source of security and helps you in your search for maturity and autonomy.

Therefore it is necessary to rediscover that "natural parenthood" of your parents which is a gift of God. They are the instruments or administrators of a parenthood which is far above them and us.

"Will you accept children lovingly from God, and bring them up according to the law of Christ and his Church?" This question is asked of the man and woman who present themselves before the altar to consecrate their love in marriage.

We can't deny that once this gift has been received many parents are either irresponsible or simply incapable of administering it.

"The trouble with people is not that they are bad but that they are ignorant," Martin Luther King used to say.

Everyone, even an adult, needs to be educated and formed in his or her responsibilities, not so much professional responsibilities as human ones. But we learn together, making mistakes together and beginning again together.

My wish is that in your family there may be that dialogue, that minimum of communication necessary in order to feel united, mutually protected and happy. I especially hope that, on your part, you may appreciate that motherhood/fatherhood which is exercised—even if poorly—with an affection which nature watches over and continually nourishes.

Don't forget that God reveals himself to our hearts even in ways outside the ordinary—in this case, through the family.

"Who are my father and my mother?"

The necessary answer brings you to contemplate the fatherhood/motherhood of God as supreme, totally trustworthy, far stronger and more generous than any other. In the daily search for him, we discover that we are children who are truly loved.

"But Zion said, 'The Lord has forsaken me, my Lord has forgotten me.' Can a woman forget her sucking child, that she should have no compassion on the son of her womb? Even these may forget, yet I will not forget you" (Is 49:14-15).

In this brief and simple document of faith is hidden God's loving care for each human person. To be aware of this love, to never stop believing in it, we need to draw near to it each day in silence, and in the moments of community worship.

The "Father" and Fathers

When St. Francis of Assisi was spending his inheritance on good works, his father, Peter Bernardone, asked him to stop and restore to him what was left. This was to be done in the presence of the bishop.

Francis willingly agreed. When the meeting took place, the young man took off his fine clothes and handed them to his father. "Until now," he said, "I have called you my father on earth. From now on I can say with full trust, 'Our Father who art in heaven,' since I have placed all my treasure, my trust and my hope in him."

Deeply moved, the bishop embraced Francis, covered him with his own robe and asked his servants to find something for the young man to clothe himself with.

St. Alphonsus de Liguori, a twenty-five-year-old public official of the eighteenth century, has left us an example of respect and self-control with regard to his father, Joseph, a military official who was very irascible and proud.

One evening, the Liguoris held a brilliant reception. When it was time for the guests to leave, one of the servants was not at the door on time to provide light with his torch. This defect in etiquette wounded the commander's self-love. As soon as the ladies and gentlemen had left, Don Joseph took the servant aside and angrily reproved him as if he had committed a crime. He walked back and forth, cursing and reproaching him for the incident. Alphonsus felt sorry for the poor servant. At a certain point he couldn't refrain himself any longer. "Father," he exclaimed, "when you begin, you never finish!"

The observation was too correct to be borne. Alphonsus was near his father's hand and received a resounding slap. Without saying a word, the young man went to his room. At supper time his place was empty. His mother went to his room to call him, and found him in tears before his crucifix. Was he upset over the insult he had suffered? Over his father's brutality? No; he was upset because he had lacked in respect toward his father. "Mother, I was wrong. Please ask him to forgive me!" Together they went to the hot-tempered officer. The son humbled himself, and the father, secretly ashamed and glad to get out of the situation, embraced him and blessed him.

For Reflection

Francis and Alphonsus, whom the Church offers as models of Christian life, seem to respond differently to the question: "Who is my father?" And yet both of them, each according to his own situation, manifest a profound awareness that God is the Father of all fatherhood, the One who calls the human person to an absolute love, a love without compromise. What do you think?

Try to find for each of these episodes a passage from the Gospel (or another part of the Bible) to which you can link the behavior of Francis and Alphonsus.

In your daily choices, what value do you attribute to the advice of your parents?

If your choice of a path in life is contrary to the expectations of your parents, how will you handle this, or how have you done so? What criteria will you be guided by?

A Communion to be Created

Reading Life

"Yes to marriage...." So read a newspaper headline on February 5, 1990.

The article read in part:

"The 'single' is leaving the scene. He was the protagonist of the eighties, celebrated and envied, happy to boast of his freedom. Now he tiptoes away from his fans, who are convinced that they can identify with him.... He discovers that only the married life, so despised in past years, can provide happiness. It doesn't enslave. It guarantees serenity."

Clearly this isn't only a matter of faith but of good sense first of all.

Far from deceiving ourselves that everyone has suddenly been converted to Catholic moral teaching, we should rather believe that, after having touched bottom, many persons are reconsidering the undoubted advantages of a stable union.

For a father and mother to be honored, they need to create the necessary conditions.

When I speak with young people, especially in confession, I always ask information about the family.

"Do your parents get along?"

"Well, they argue every once in a while."

"Sometimes they quarrel."

When someone has to say that his or her parents are separated or divorced, there is always a moment of hesitation, a kind of strange fear. It's understandable if we think that the young person is either ashamed of revealing it or is even experiencing a sense of guilt.

The "why" is mysterious. "Maybe I didn't do everything I should have. Maybe they did it because of me, to make me suffer less...."

There's no doubt: before being father and mother, a couple is called to be man and woman, husband and wife. The stability of the family rests essentially on their availability, capability and clarity of ideas. It is measured against what they desire, against what they believe.

Do we want to place the whole blame on them?

Certainly not.

But we do need to note that, unfortunately many parents lack balance and miss the goal.

To look after the children, take on heavy responsibilities for them, and then forget that nothing can replace a tranquil, serene atmosphere of dialogue in the family, is like deceiving ourselves that we can lift a house with our fingers when we haven't taken care of our rheumatism.

John Paul II writes:

"The family is the first and fundamental school of social living; as a community of love, it finds in self-giving the law that guides it and makes it grow. The self-giving that inspires the love of husband and wife for each other is the model and norm for the self-giving that must be practiced in the relationships between brothers and sisters and the different generations living together in the family. And the communion and sharing that are part of everyday life in the home at times of joy and at times of difficulty are the most concrete and effective pedagogy for the active, responsible and fruitful inclusion of the children in the wider horizon of society."[2]

The gift of self!

This is the lifestyle which, on the day of their marriage, the future father and mother pledged themselves to realize.

This isn't only a religious fulfillment of the will of God, but a form of pedagogy, an educational method, so that the children born of that gift may, in turn, be able to give, to share, to live for others, as they have seen it done in their family.

And this style, this manner of being, this absolutely primary choice, is much more important to the growth of the children than many other useless acts of generosity, which often manifest—instead of generosity—egoism, the desire for gratification, and therefore a subtle will to dominate.

Listening to the Word

"It is not good that the man should be alone; I will make him a helper fit for him" (Gen 2:18).

God's plan for the human couple and the very institution of marriage is forever based on this passage.

So as not to consider only the "institutional" aspect of the life of the married couple, with the possible risk of lessening one's understanding of how much joy and love there is for man and woman in this plan, it is helpful to read carefully chapters one and two of the book of Genesis, not seeing them as a history or a chronicle of the early ages, but as a testimony of faith: God creates, he shares his life because he loves; man and woman are the highest, most significant symbol of how God works with love on behalf of humankind.

The Old Testament is rich in accounts of the goodness God shows to married couples.

Certainly, marriage may also become the object of pacts or exchanges not exactly suggested by love and the desire for fidelity (cf. Lev 18:6-19, or Deut 25:5-10). But it is enough to read the Song of Songs to be aware that in God's plan the joy and passion of union flee from social constrictions and require a just freedom. The most beautiful passages from this book are 1:1-4; 2:8; 3:4; 4:1-15; 5:10-16; 8:5-7.

The book of Tobit also presents a genuine, faithful love that resists the troubles of life, a chaste love that is sustained by the faith of Sarah and Tobiah, who know how to blend what greatly attracts persons in their mutual communion, that is, the union of body, with what unites them more profoundly with God, that is, the spontaneous prayer of praise and request for help.

In the New Testament the communion between man and woman becomes more demanding because it is assured by God. What Moses had allowed "for...hardness of heart," Jesus restores to God's original plan: "What, therefore, God has joined together, let not man put asunder" (Mt 19:6, 8).

In the language of the Gospel this means: it's no use to say, "If I no longer feel up to it, it's better to quit." Even when the heart is under the influence of egoism, it can always draw from that treasure called "the grace of God."

This means that you can't simply hide behind the defects of your character or justify yourself by saying that you aren't a saint. Saints, that is, persons who are capable of carrying out God's will, are persons who humbly follow God and let themselves be formed gradually by him.

Jesus not only restores marriage to its condition in the original plan of God, but he gives it a special dignity. He makes it an extraordinarily meaningful symbol of his own love for his followers.

He becomes the "Spouse of the Church"; he loves her, nourishes her and cares for her, as each man is called to do for his wife.

And so the first Christian marriage is that between Jesus and the Church (cf. Eph 5:25-33).

This total, absolute self-giving serves as a model for every other union that, by free choice, takes place "in church," that is, in the presence of God.

If You Wish to Grow

Full communion in your family depends on everyone, including you.

We often forget that communion is a gift of God. Therefore we need to ask for it and then receive it as a gift.

It requires, in fact demands, the ability, the *courage* to pause together in order to be aware that the God in whom we believe is present. He is there and he asks to be listened to, recognized and placed at the center.

It's much too easy to take refuge behind the alibi of the hurried schedule of daily life. Most of the time we are the ones who create the pace. Behind all the rushing we can find some egoism, a need to feel committed and to do many things, some of which are useless or excessive, in order to escape what is essential.

Communication requires time and space!

First of all, communication with God.

Perhaps it's too much to ask you to pray together with the members of your family, especially if you've never done it before. But you could suggest some simple moments of prayer: for example, prayer before meals; the reading of a passage from Scripture in the evening, even that of the liturgy of the Word from the following day; or other forms suited to the seasons of the year, such as prayer around the nativity scene.

Am I suggesting ridiculous things? Perhaps, if the Christian faith is absurd. And even more if it is absurd to believe that, in the family, the Christian faith should be manifested as the faith of a community, as salvation to be welcomed together.

Then, *interpersonal communication*.

Cardinal Martini writes: "The difficulty in communicating in the husband-wife relationship and in the parent-child relationship (after the children have reached a certain age)

is so proverbial that we admire as happy exceptions those couples or those parents who say they have no problems in this regard. In fact, on this point we believe that they have little credibility, that they desire to give a different appearance to what instead is the daily struggle that we all experience. And yet it would be possible to notably improve the web of communication within the family if only we wanted to believe one another more and to invest a bit more effort on a point that is essential for health and joy in life."[3]

And John Paul II writes:

"Faced with a society that is running the risk of becoming more and more depersonalized and standardized and therefore inhuman and dehumanizing, with the negative results of many forms of escapism—such as alcoholism, drugs and even terrorism—the family possesses and continues still to release formidable energies capable of taking man out of his anonymity, keeping him conscious of his personal dignity, enriching him with deep humanity and actively placing him, in his uniqueness and unrepeatability, within the fabric of society."[4]

It is an undeniable fact that the family, as it is called to be a "school of sociability," can become the initial cause of individualism, of an intellectual, ideal and even religious individualism.

Why in so many families is verbal communication used solely to communicate trivial things?

It's true that the gap between the various ways of understanding life makes itself felt. However, it should be possible to fill it to some extent, or at least to attempt to discover, behind the reactions of the parents, some basic thoughts, some life styles on which you feel you can all agree.

Have you ever reflected on the value of "signs"?

A sign is defined simply as "something that stands for something else." The flower, the sweater, the box of candy that you give, the telephone call you make, the birthday that you don't forget, the care you show...all this has not only "functional" value (that is, value that lies solely in the use made of it), but is above all a sign. Through it you communicate something; or you break the circle of lack of communication which is tightening around your family. You restore the possibility of a dialogue which perhaps seemed somewhat compromised.

Reflect on how necessary it is to use our energies for this purpose.

We Belong to One Another Forever

"God is guiding your marriage. Marriage is more than your love for each other. It has a higher dignity and power, for it is God's holy ordinance, through which he wills to perpetuate the human race till the end of time. In your love you see only your two selves in the world, but in marriage you are a link in the chain of the generations, which God causes to come and to pass away to his glory, and calls into his kingdom. In your love you see only the heaven of your own happiness, but in marriage you are placed at a post of responsibility towards the world and mankind. Your love is your own private possession, but marriage is more than something personal—it is status, an office. Just as it is the crown, and not merely the will to rule, that makes the king, so it is marriage, and not merely your love for each other, that joins you together in the sight of God and man. As you first give the ring to one another and have now received it a second time from the hand of the pastor, so love comes from you, but marriage from above, from God. As high as God is above man, so high are the sanctity, the rights, and the promise of marriage above the sanctity, the rights, and the promise of love.

"God makes your marriage indissoluble. 'What therefore God has joined together, let no man put asunder' (Matt 19:6ff.). God joins you together in marriage; it is his act, not yours. Do not confound your love for one another with God. God makes your marriage indissoluble, and protects it from every danger that may threaten it from within and without; he wills to be the guarantor of its indissolubility. It is a blessed thing to know that no power on earth, no temptation, no human frailty can dissolve what God holds together; indeed, anyone who knows that may say confidently: What God has joined together *can* no man put asunder. Free from all the anxiety that is always a characteristic of love, you can now say to each other with complete and confident assurance: We can never lose each other now; by the will of God we belong to each other till death."[5]

For Reflection

This author, who died in a Nazi concentration camp, seems to propose a love that is free from the immaturity of adolescence and conscious of the responsibility it brings, of the imbalances it must be freed of, of the goals it sets for itself.

This is a good opportunity to look at the demanding proposal of an indissoluble love, that is, one resistant to the humors, whims and strange desires of freedom that often hide under a subtle egoism.

It's Wonderful to Drink from this Pitcher!

"There is an aluminum pitcher. It's old, good and shiny. The handle is broken, but this gives it the appearance of an antique. The eleven children, from the oldest to the youngest, have drunk from it. It has accompanied the family as they moved from place to place. From the country to the village, from the village to the city, from the city to the metropolis. There were births. There were deaths. The pitcher took part in everything, it always came with us. It is the continuity of the mystery of life in the diverse situations of life and death. It remains, always polished and antique. I believe that when I go home, the pitcher will already be old, with the kind of 'oldness' that is youthfulness because it generates life. It has a central place in the kitchen. Whenever you drink from that pitcher you don't drink water; you drink the freshness, the sweetness, the familiarity, the family story, the remembrances of the eager child slaking his or her thirst. It could be any kind of water. In this pitcher, it is always fresh and good. At home everyone who is thirsty drinks from this pitcher. It's like a ritual. They all exclaim: It's wonderful to drink from this pitcher! How good the water is!...

"The son returns. He has traveled around the world and has studied. He comes back. He kisses his mother and hugs his brothers and sisters. All our sorrow at his absence is gone. The words are few, and we look at one another at great length. We have to 'drink' the other first in order to love him. The eyes that drink are the language of the heart. Only after our first look at someone, can our lips speak of superficial things: How big you've gotten! How well you look! How tall you've grown! Our eyes do not speak about this; they speak of love. Only the light understands. 'Mom, I'm thirsty. I would like a drink from the old pitcher....'

"Why is the water from the pitcher good, sweet, healthy and fresh? Because the pitcher is a sacrament. The pitcher-sacrament gives the water goodness, sweetness, freshness and health."[6]

> ## For Reflection
>
> This author recounts his return from Europe to his home in Brazil. The pitcher he speaks of is the sign of the continuity of the family; it is one of the signs of family unity.
>
> Why don't you try to find something in your home that symbolically expresses continuity and unity? Why don't you try to give it a meaning, or to evaluate what meaning already exists?
>
> If your family is too young to have "contained" something in its "memory," try to create a "sign" that can be for each of you a call to greater communion.

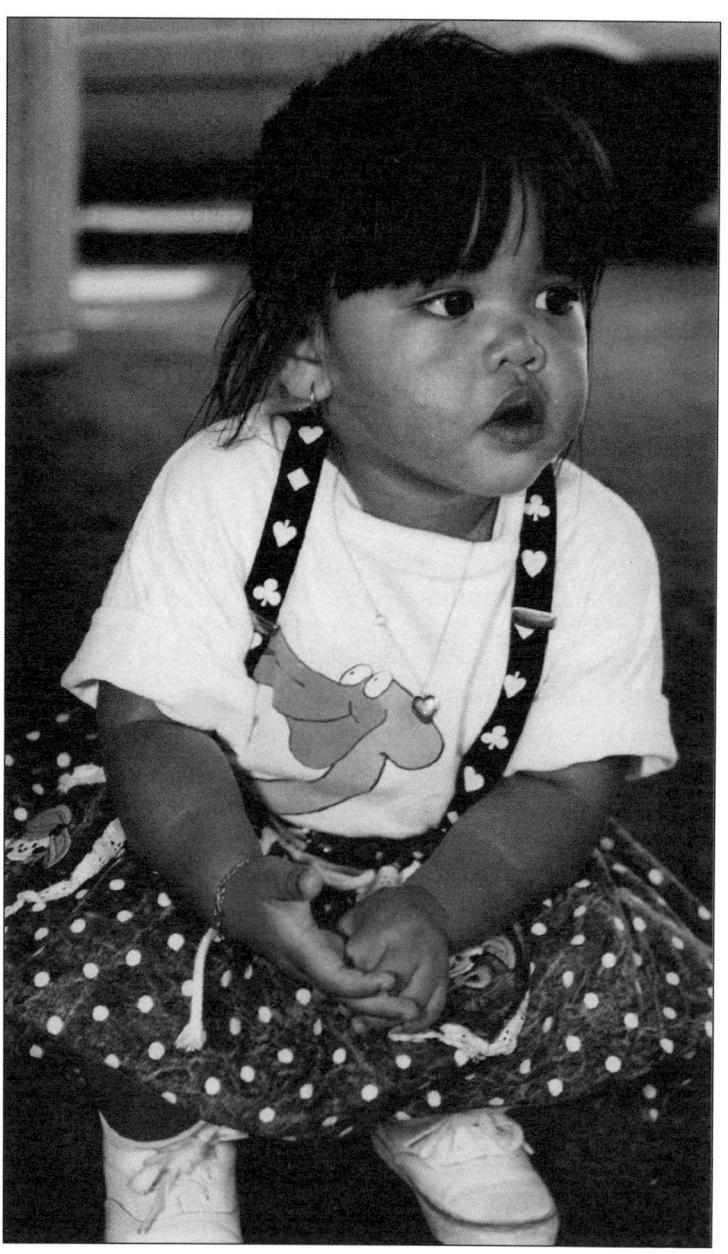

A Communion to Multiply

Reading Life

"Reduce the use of fossil fuels, make use of recycling, fight population growth, eliminate meat as food."

These are some of the principal "commandments" contained in a report of the Worldwatch Institute, the center for environmental research which has compiled a kind of check-up on the condition of the planet earth each year, from 1984 on.

The columnist who cites the report adds: "With regard to population growth (each year the planet has to support a burden of 85 to 90 million more persons) it is to be resolved, on every continent, by a strict control of births."

Poor planet! It has to support its children, the children of that life thanks to which the planet itself exists!

So we humans must save ourselves by consuming less fuel, eating less meat, having fewer children.... The experts undoubtedly are clear and, it seems, don't have too many scruples. Children are as dangerous as fuel and a piece of beef. And, once the meat is eliminated and there are more cows and oxen, the lot of human beings still does not look rosy. For they, more than their animal friends, have become the "unjust aggressors," and so are to be eliminated or simply avoided.

Don't fail to compare your attitude with the above attitude. Be afraid of yourself if, in conscience, you think the same way. You can't pretend to be unaware that, if the problem is so catastrophic, it's because thirty percent of the countries on this planet exploit the resources of the remaining seventy percent. Yet, despite this injustice, they are neither happy nor satisfied. They forget that, if equitably distributed, the earth's resources would be enough for everyone.

Might not the day come when we will no longer honor father and mother, simply because it will be more difficult to find a father and mother? Perhaps the day will come (or has already come) when we will be accustomed to thinking that we are alive, not thanks to an act of love, but rather as the result of a game of chance, because of which we have come on a scene that rejects us and wants nothing more than our disappearance.

"Cursed be the day on which I was born! The day on which my mother bore me, let it not be blessed! Cursed be the man who brought the news to my father, 'A son is born to you,' making him very glad" (Jer 20:14-15).

At the height of his interior suffering, even the prophet Jeremiah curses his existence.

But what is more frightening in our present culture is the absolute lack of inhibition, the tranquil moral indifference with which the life of human persons is considered a limitation, an obstacle to the security of everyone else, to the security of a few.

Perhaps less frightening is the attitude of many desperate women, represented by Claudia Cardinale who, in the film *Act of Sorrow*, kills her own son.

"A widow, wearied by a life of problems and struggles.... One day this woman discovered that her son was a drug addict; she tried to help him with every possible means, with much affection. And then to her the only, sad, radical solution left seemed to be to kill her son, who had become a derelict."

This is how the actress described the character she played.

Here, in this situation, the mother undoubtedly neither hates nor is indifferent to the life of her son. She accepts the suffering, then in an act of desperation mixed with egoism, she kills her son, as if to restore to him a dignity beyond human life.

Since it is true that to love is to suffer for those we love, it is inevitable that to be a father and mother demands suffering for those who were given life through love.

Listening to the Word

Does God suffer?

Some theologians are horrified at the image that this question creates. They correctly affirm: God is God, so he cannot suffer. Creatures suffer because they are creatures, but the Creator, never.

But the Bible gives us many images of God in which the equation love = suffering seems true even for God.

With the passion typical of parenthood, the God of Israel participates in the troubles, sorrows and sins of his people.

"Return, faithless Israel, says the Lord. I will not look on you in anger, for I am merciful, says the Lord; I will not be angry for ever" (Jer 3:12).

Or again:

"I have seen the affliction of my people who are in Egypt, and have heard their cry because of their taskmasters; indeed, I know their sufferings" (Ex 3:7).

Or:

"The Lord is near to the brokenhearted, and saves the crushed in spirit" (Ps 34:18).

But the high point of this loving-suffering is found in Jesus Christ, and it lies precisely in his being son and in accepting the will of the Father. There is no more beautiful or convincing expression of this suffering than that which St. Paul offers in Philippians 2:5-11.

The unanimous testimony of the word of God is this: God is love, and for this reason he has us call him "Father."

In his family, communion is nourished continually, for all are his children and all are called to be aware of this truth.

"Love your enemies, and do good, and lend, expecting nothing in return; and your reward will be great, and you will be sons of the Most High" (Lk 6:35).

"But when the time had fully come, God sent forth his Son, born of woman, born under the law, to redeem those who were under the law, so that we might receive adoption as sons. And because you are sons, God has sent the Spirit of his Son into our hearts, crying, 'Abba! Father!' So through God you are no longer a slave but a son, and if a son then an heir" (Gal 4:4-7).

Silently contemplate this truthful image! God does not limit himself to "wanting children," but acts in such a way that we feel ourselves to be his children.

And add this: "See what love the Father has given us, that we should be called children of God; and so we are" (1 Jn 3:1).

The family of God is enriched with new children, each loved as a person, adopted—that is, welcomed—each taken in his/her dignity without threats or conditions.

Man and woman are called to be father and mother in the name of God, as instruments of God. To be against life is to be against God. To be doubtful, withdrawn, intolerant, insipid, indifferent toward new life is the same as to disobey or fail to be friends with God.

The most beautiful pages of the Bible on this topic are those in which God frees from their misery those women who desired children and could not have them.

There is the story of Samuel and his mother Hannah (1 Sam 1:1-2, 11).

Directly linked to the birth of Jesus, there is the story of Mary's cousin Elizabeth (Lk 1:5-25, 39-79).

If You Wish to Grow

To learn the power of the commandment we are speaking of means to learn how to be a parent.

Perhaps some parents have never stopped "playing" at being parents. To be a parent entails more than "bearing." It means "to bring forth, to give birth to." To bring forth to life, not just once but continually. To bring forth a life that is not only a biological body, but a dynamism to be discovered with patience and, once discovered, to be loved and protected. It is a dynamism that leads to dialogue, emerging from one's own securities, to letting oneself be formed, without presumption.

Many young people have difficulty in bringing forth.

It's easier, more gratifying to let oneself be carried, even transported; to avoid responsibilities, to pretend not to feel the call to life; to find excuses, because to be a father or mother we need so much that we're not ready for yet.... We'll think about it!

If you wish to grow, and to grow as a Christian, don't forget that the event of our salvation was born of an act of acceptance of maternity. Mary the Mother of Jesus did not count as much on her own strength as on the "Don't be afraid" with which God assured her through the words of an angel.

Certainly, we can't take the fear away from the human person in a psychological sense, but we can help him or her to hope, to recover his/her moral strength. We must not leave people to their desperation.

In certain families, the relationships are so tense, so false, as to have us believe that none of the children will want to repeat the same experience of family life.

We need to learn how to take risks and restore solidarity.

In your family you can give something more, so that in our world fatherhood and motherhood will not be considered an impossible undertaking or a useless sacrifice.

Can't We Build Bridges?

"I think that friendship between father and son is certainly difficult but not unattainable. I've succeeded in getting along pretty well with my parents. Too often we young people are reluctant to confide in our family members and this has a negative effect on the possibility for confidence. But it's also true that once we've reached a certain age all of us feel self-sufficient; we want to prepare ourselves to solve difficult problems alone. And it's only when we hit our heads against a wall more than once that we remember that we have a mother and father. Unfortunately, parents often have only a patriarchal view of the family, where the father commands and the children obey. This makes friendship very difficult and raises barriers. And if this is how it is, why condemn them? They act this way because they believe it is the best method for educating children. And if they don't let their children go out at night, it's because they feel it's for the best.

"We should be more loving, better behaved and kinder, to be able to gain their trust. This isn't so hard. And if some evening a parent doesn't feel up to a discussion, we young people should realize that our father may have some problems at work. We must realize that our parents have their own problems. Those instead who have parents ready to become their friends should treasure them, not just trying to get money out of them or a clean shirt, and then getting angry if they ask us why we look sad. Our father is not a money-keeper nor our mother a maid. After all, they're the ones who brought us into this world, raised us, fed us, and gave us everything so we might not lack anything!

"This alone should be enough to keep a son or daughter close to father and mother."

(Letter from a young man to a TV station)

For Reflection

This letter is certainly very positive, if for no other reason than the young man's effort to value the good he has received from his parents. Do you appreciate the actions or disposition of your parents? Are you able to tell them so? If at times there is something to clarify or point out, how do you go about it? Like a bulldozer or a hoe?...

In addition, this young man is grateful to life. He accepts his own reality and implicitly rejects harmful utopias or flight into unreal worlds. Such false worlds are a direct cause of the destruction of family relationships. Do you think it's possible to relaunch the acceptance of life on the basis of a better relationship between parents and children?

Do you think it's true that many adults develop an anti-life mentality because they feel defrauded of the affection and recognition of their children?

Aren't Two Parents Enough?

Reading Life

The question is provocative: how many fathers and mothers should you honor? It's a provocative question, but not a useless one.

A recent survey of some young people preparing for marriage revealed that they looked forward to forming a common project for their life together. It also revealed that a large percentage of young couples believe that marriage is indissoluble—a common life project, founded on the certainty that what has been joined together can't be separated.

But, as we know, other statistics reveal the opposite. Indissolubility becomes a stand that is less and less convincing, even though indissolubility is not downplayed at the moment of the wedding.

Indissolubility calls for a strong desire for stability and fidelity, together with readiness to make sacrifices. These attitudes sustain the moral choices and the big and small decisions on which the durability of a marriage is founded. In this awareness the choice of faith must be present. Outside the Christian and religious sphere it is hard for a couple to be convinced that indissolubility is not an excessive burden, that it is not irrelevant to our times.

In the break-up of family unity, the children are the ones who suffer most, and through no fault of their own.

Aren't two parents enough?

If we were to judge by many cases, the answer would be *no*.

Today many young people spend a major part of their adolescence divided between mothers who have remarried and fathers who are "making a new life for themselves."

Mark, a fourteen-year-old, says:

"I hate my father; he left us to go with another woman when I was eight years old and really needed him. But, I don't know how to explain it, I still love him, because he's my father. Sometimes at night, when I'm in bed, I think about him and I want to hug him...."

Katie, a girl who attempted suicide because of her family situation, comments:

"The worst thing for me is that when I'm with my mom, she speaks badly of my father and tells me why it's wrong for me to love him. And instead, when I'm with my father, he tells me what a monster my mother is and how much I should hate her. I love both of them, but when I try to tell them how I feel, they look at me angrily as if I had betrayed their affection. If I think about these things, I become so sad and confused that I shut myself up in my room and cry."

These words are a sad confirmation of the unhappy situation of many teenagers. Young people tossed between their parents, who often have new spouses, may find it hard to become balanced. These realities point to a culture in which everything that is pleasing is desirable and therefore licit and possible. As the philosopher Emmanuel Levinas says, it's not what is a value that is desirable; rather, what is desirable becomes a value.

Listening to the Word

We have already seen that the Bible contains objective truth concerning the indissolubility of marriage.

Even stronger are the words that the inspired writers address to the various forms of imbalance that can be found within the married life, threatening the mutual fidelity of the couple. In general these faults are categorized as "adultery."

The Old Testament clearly condemns the practice of polygamy, which arose from the distorted idea that fruitfulness tended to increase the power of the family (the more children, the more power).

We need only carefully read Genesis 2:18-24, to see that the biblical ideal is undoubtedly monogamy.

Unique and undivided love seems to prevail among the great biblical figures: Isaac, Joseph, Judith, Ezekiel, Job. If we read the Song of Songs, we note that the love of the two spouses, a symbol of God's love for his people, is clearly undivided. In the Old Testament, adultery violates the woman's belonging to her husband or betrothed. The woman is only the man's possession (cf. Ex 20:17).

Jesus saves the adulterous woman from the hypocritical anger of the crowd, but he condemns her sin: "Go, and do not sin again" (Jn 8:11).

With Jesus, however, woman regains her dignity. The imbalances, the temptations, the escapades of married life, are a risk, and a sin, for both the woman and the man. To the men of his time, the Lord's severity may have appeared excessive: "You have heard that it was said, 'You shall not commit adultery.' But I say to you that every one who looks at a woman lustfully has already committed adultery with her in his heart" (Mt 5:27).

This refers not just to the simple desire, but to that attitude by which a man sees a woman as an object of exploitation, of erotic gratification, and acts accordingly almost with pride, believing it to be a condition of his manhood.

However, the words of Jesus about adultery in general are severe (cf. Mt 5:31-32). And St. Paul states that the adulterer—that is, one who is so habitually and tries to justify himself—will not inherit the kingdom of God (cf. 1 Cor 6:9).

What matters for us is not only the moral condemnation contained in the Bible. What matters, instead, is that the life of Christians is to be modeled on the religious sense of the covenant with God. Everything that we do we are called to do for the Lord and not for ourselves (cf. 2 Cor 5:15). This demands a real seriousness, a serene reflection that gives a decisive character to our actions, especially those which involve our neighbor.

Jesus always shows great understanding toward sinners; we are all sinners, since the carelessness, the errors and the weaknesses of moral life cannot be permanently overcome.

The Lord's severity is directed at that systematic manner of thinking and acting that wants to isolate the conscience from the law of God which is written above all in the heart. People who base their lives on this isolation remain outside the covenant with God. There is, therefore, a real adultery with regard to one's relationship with God. It is the spouse rebelling against the spouse, pretending to have absolute freedom, which is the cause and effect of the moral evil in the world.

James states it clearly: "Unfaithful creatures! Do you not know that friendship with the world is enmity with God? Therefore whoever wishes to be a friend of the world makes himself an enemy of God" (Jas 4:4).

If You Wish to Grow

Young people with three or four parents are no longer the exception. Of course, this is only a manner of speaking. A person can have only one mother and one father, not only in the order of nature, but also as regards affective attachment.

Many parents are convinced that they made a mistake on the day of their marriage. Then, partly for their own emotional balance and partly to give the children substitute parent figures, they remarry or decide to live with other persons.

It is certainly difficult for young people to live in such situations, but often they can serve to favor a more rapid growth in maturity.

To assume the attitude of "condemnation to the end," refusing any communication with the "guilty" parent or with either parent, can be a legitimate outlet for emotions, but it's not constructive in the long run.

The future will reveal how much these tensions result in a difficult growth period for young people, a growth that is troubled and sunk in anxiety. But to create barricades doesn't help anything or anyone.

First of all, with regard to the "innocent" parent: If he or she believes, in conscience, that the children's contact with the other spouse will be negative, he/she has the duty to prevent it. But this refusal must be purified of any egoism, lack of reasonableness or lack of love. Experience tells us how difficult this is.

Then, regarding the young person:

Often these situations cause them to become opportunists: to have a father on one side and a mother on the other side easily becomes a source of emotional, then material, exploitation, with all the advantages that follow.

To say, "They deserve it," may be true, but the terrible consequences to the formation of their character are overlooked. This means that young people can turn into cynics and opportunists, without scruples. And this often results in recreating, to a greater degree, the atmosphere which produced the initial problems.

Frank, a father and religion teacher, remarks:

"Today there's a view of the family that's pretty widespread, if not in words at least in actions. The family isn't seen any longer as a center of love among its members but almost as a place of business, a place for the exchange of loans, and sometimes a place from which to draw benefits and in which to minimize the commitments and sacrifices made for one another. In short, it's an institution to be done away with when it's no longer useful, when it requires sacrifices and renunciations that are not balanced off by advantages. In fact, sometimes the family is neglected or misunderstood from the beginning and breaks apart before anyone knows what's happening. But all this has little influence in the family that has clear Christian values."

Honoring father and mother means assuming an attitude of faith; faith in the untouchable values of unity and communication. Faith in God, as a guarantee for remaining firm in these values when they seem useless or difficult.

Perhaps God permits difficulties so that greater growth and joy may result. Young persons who experience these situations can find in them opportunities for strengthening these values within themselves and for developing trust in the One who does nothing by chance, but always reveals his Providence toward the afflicted and needy.

Views
The Child of...Several Parents

A teacher writes:

"I'm a junior-high teacher. This year I came to know the family situations of some of my students. I know that some of their parents are separated or divorced, or are having a serious disagreement. I'd be grateful if you would help me better understand this sad reality that so many of my students are living...."

An expert responds:

"For the child, especially a very young one, it is very hard to distinguish between his relationship with the parents and the parents' relationship with one another. If the latter alters, the child will conclude that the first has altered also.... This easily causes a feeling of guilt in the teen or child who often, in seeing the attention given him/her decrease, believes he/she is in some way the cause of the conflict between his/her parents....

"These children do not have models to refer to. Often they feel rejected by at least one parent. They feel abandoned; they have seen the mother or father go out with another man or woman. They have suffered physical or psychological abuse, or they find themselves living with a new father or mother, even with new brothers and sisters. The absence of a positive relationship between the parents, or the presence of a negative parent figure, create the lack of a role model and a model of identification, a lack that makes their balanced growth and their attainment of a clear personal identity more difficult.... After separation or even after divorce the conflicts can increase.... To obtain the trust of the child is a sign of victory over the former spouse.... In this conflict the child is only the object of competition.... Educators need to learn the art of entering the reality of their students. Confidence, which is the key for entering into a person's heart, cannot be forced; one can only obtain it by showing oneself truly capable of understanding the other...."[7]

For Reflection

The picture of the situation, as given in this reply, is truly harsh. Do you agree with it?

What would you say to parents who hastily decide to separate, without giving much consideration to their children?

What would you say to a friend who finds him/herself in this situation?

Honor Until the Expiration Date?

Reading Life

This is a somewhat biased question: does the fourth commandment have an expiration date? Is there a time limit beyond which we no longer have to "honor" but can rather "neglect"?

There is no doubt that for some persons there is a strong temptation to obey the commandment "neglect your father and your mother."

This topic often arises in disputes about morality: can there be a form of life toward which legal obligations and moral duties cease, leaving us the freedom to do what we want with the elderly? Some people seem to think this way.

Here is one author's analysis of how this mentality has come about: "Among the factors for the change in attitude toward death, and consequently for people's behavior toward it, we include modern industrial society which, according to Max Weber, is to be interpreted in the light of two fundamental categories: rationality and efficiency. These categories have an immediate repercussion on the interpretation of death. A world largely dominated by magic categories or at least by non-rational categories and categories directed to the other world, is gradually being replaced by a society built completely on reason and based totally on earth. It is a reason that is not so much philosophical as instrumental, placed at the service of production, of industrial production. We are in the kingdom of the budget, of programming, and of experimentation: that is, of rationality and efficiency."[8]

This is a very clear analysis and one to be shared. While it doesn't make sense to return to magic because it belongs to the realm of the irrational, we cannot forget that the efficiency model of present society contributes to the marginalization of all who produce little or nothing. Among these are elderly parents.

They are often seen as a difficult burden to bear.

It's hard to find a family into which they will be respected and integrated. It's hard for the children to make the grandchildren accept them. It's hard to find the economic means to assist them, to "support them."

When they *are* shown respect, may it not be chiefly for the inheritance which sooner or later will be passed on—respected, therefore, as a form of advantageous investment?

Listening to the Word

In the Old Testament, a long life represents the natural hope of those who are happy and possess many goods. But the prospect of old age looks very different to someone who is experiencing unhappiness and is abandoned by everyone.

"O death, how bitter is the reminder of you to one who lives at peace among his possessions, to a man without distractions, who is prosperous in everything, and who still has the vigor to enjoy his food! O death, how welcome is your sentence to one who is in need and is failing in strength, very old and distracted over everything; to one who is contrary, and has lost patience!" (Sir 41:1-2)

This sentence is truly bitter. It certainly can be placed on the lips of many elderly parents who have been abandoned by their children.

Scripture urges young and middle-aged men and women not to neglect the care of their own parents: "Honor your father and your mother, that your days may be long in the land which the Lord your God gives you" (Ex 20:12).

One of the greatest joys we can give our parents is to enable them to become serene grandparents: "Grandchil-

dren are the crown of the aged, and the glory of sons is their fathers" (Prov 17:6).

The commandment is expressed in a more severe but profoundly human form, like this: "O son, help your father in his old age, and do not grieve him as long as he lives; even if he is lacking in understanding, show forbearance; in all your strength do not despise him. For kindness to a father will not be forgotten, and against your sins it will be credited to you; in the day of your affliction it will be remembered in your favor; as frost in fair weather, your sins will melt away. Whoever forsakes his father is like a blasphemer, and whoever angers his mother is cursed by the Lord" (Sir 3:12-16).

The Gospels do not directly address the theme of respect for the aged parent. However, Jesus has one of his tremendous clashes with the Pharisees over the interpretation of a human law, according to which it becomes conveniently possible to neglect one's duty toward one's parents (cf. Mk 7:1-13).

We cannot deny that it is from the "elders" of the people (that is, some of the religious authorities of the time, cf. Mt 16:21) that Jesus experienced the greatest hostility. Nor should we ignore the fact that Jesus' attitude toward his family was marked by a great interior freedom, which also became a freedom of movement, as the needs of the kingdom of God require. Jesus' radical choice was expressed in his leaving his family and giving up his own home. He advised his disciples to do likewise (cf. Mt 19:10-12). Nevertheless, it is still true that the entire Bible inspires a sentiment of great respect toward those who have given us life.

In my opinion, in Jesus' life we especially find this expressed in the episode of the mother at the foot of the cross. From this event, Christian tradition has drawn the certainty that there is and will always be a spiritual maternity exercised by Mary toward all Christians and all people, for whom Jesus died (cf. Jn 19:25-27).

A great student of John's Gospel, J. de la Potterie writes:

"Mary's presence at the foot of the cross has been variously interpreted. Today an ever increasing number of exegetes recognize that this scene shows not only an act of filial piety toward his mother on Jesus' part, but a real revelation of her spiritual motherhood. Two important arguments support this interpretation. First of all, contrary to his usual practice, Jesus calls his mother "woman...." She is therefore no longer only the mother of Jesus.... In addition, the account follows a literary form called a schema of revelation; the words of Jesus reveal a mystery: Mary here becomes the mother, not only of the beloved disciple, but of all those whom he represents, the sum total of all believers."[9]

If You Wish to Grow

"Honor your father and your mother. To honor means much more than to love. The relationship between parents and children is not symmetrical. Whatever their age and ours, their knowledge and ours, we can never forget that we received life from them. Here lies the hidden greatness that places them above us. To honor means to recognize this fact and this greatness. The fourth commandment is inserted in a religious context which makes us see our parents as mediators of a life that comes from God. To honor our parents in this way is to make an act of faith. Only faith enables us to see in our parents the sign and witness of the gifts of God. Today we often find young people who, instead of thanking their parents for the gift of life, reprove them for having brought them into the world. In a secularized culture, outside of a religious context, it's no longer clear that persons see their lives as something good, as a gift." [10]

Could it be that—as Pesch writes—because we no longer love life, we no longer love those through whom that life came to us? Is this a clumsy and desperate cry of vengeance regarding the fatherhood of God?

Will we, too, be the children and slaves of Nietzsche's cry: "God is dead! And we have killed him!"?

As human beings we can't help evaluating, discerning, remembering. At a certain age it's normal to start criticizing the mistakes of our parents. We become aware that many of our imbalances and problems depend on them and on their love, which may have been weak and/or too indulgent, upset by ignorance, presumption, inability to share in the difficulties of the children, and inability or lack of will to dialogue or understand the present time.

We especially reason this way when our parents are older. Because we children have grown and matured and are more intelligent, it takes little for us to mercilessly call up the past.

As human beings and as Christians, our memory should be at peace. If forgiveness is needed, it should arise from an awareness that everyone makes mistakes and that children very often repeat the same errors with their own children, for to err is human.

The elderly person needs greater affection. This affection should be genuine and not given only for the sake of consoling. It should be capable of overcoming resistance. It should be an expression of love for life, however it manifests itself, even in sickness and suffering. This affection should spring from the "inversion" of roles, by which children become the "parents" of their own parents, and return the attention, love and care that they themselves received, even if they don't think they received these.

Views

What Else Can the Fourth Commandment Mean Today?

A Check to Pay the Rent....

I spoke with a mother who is advanced in age.

Time has not erased the traces of a rare beauty on her face, but there are also traces of deep sorrow. Caused by whom?

By her son. He has a good position; he bought himself a huge house; but there is no room for his mother!

He also bought a dog, one of those "ornamental" dogs which are quite expensive because they are so rare. The dog eats three pounds of meat a day. And the mother?

His mother asked if he would at least pay the modest rent for her small apartment, which she reaches by climbing a long flight of stairs. The son answered, "How can I, mother? I can't do it!"

...Or a basket of fresh fruit

A few days later I was talking to a man in his sixties. He lives in two small rooms, one upstairs and one downstairs. To get from one room to another, he has to go outside, even in the damp cold of winter.

His daughter has a beautiful home, with a luxurious garden that produces flowers and fruit. Every so often she sends a basket of fruit to the sisters who run the nursery that her small son attends.

But for ten years the grandfather has been waiting for a gesture like this—the gift of some fruit from his daughter. Do you think he has ever received it? Never.

I saw the poor man cry. "I did so much for my daughter!..."[11]

For Reflection

These stories were not fabricated. Situations such as these (and even worse) are becoming more widespread, for an endless number of reasons. Look around you. Perhaps something like this is happening close by. In a group, try to evaluate how much of this situation is to be attributed to today's society and how much to neglect and selfishness on the part of individuals.

Read Exodus 20:1-17. Pause on verse 12 and reflect on the importance God attributes to the observance of his "Word," remembering how much value the Israelites placed on a long life.

Roots

A young woman named Christine habitually attracted my attention because of her clear gaze and gentle face. She had such an air of nobility and grace.

But, as Christmas drew near her habitual graciousness vanished. She seemed far away, and if she smiled, the smile contained a touch of bitterness. One day I went to visit her in her small house, made beautiful by its order and a touch of elegance. With evident suffering she shared with me her deep pain. She showed me a small roll of paper that had yellowed with age and was wrapped in a piece of ugly material. I read it. "Today, December 15, I give my daughter Christine to whomever finds her. The baby is one month old." The text was written in irregular handwriting and the signature was almost unrecognizable. Christine had been abandoned by her mother on one of the poorest streets of the area. A married couple had found her on their way home from a day's work in the fields. They had no children and they received little Christine, half dead from the cold, as a blessing from heaven. With great sacrifice they raised her and sent her to school; she became one of the most admired young women of the village and among the first to attend a university.

After having cared for Christine with a selflessness that transcended blood relationship, the adoptive mother died, leaving the girl that one indication about her family.

After trying to envision her own mother for years, Christine had thus been able to find her—old, sick and worn out by a life of wanderings, even though she had come from a very good family.

Christine found her in a hospital. When she arrived near her mother's bed, the woman was asleep. Was this the face that she had dreamed about a thousand times since she was a child, while lying beneath her rough woolen blanket? Were those the features she had attempted to trace with her finger on the windows of the old kitchen? Was this the woman who had given the daughter such a strong passion for her family, despite her own empty and disordered life?

The old woman opened her eyes and looked at the girl for a long time before asking her, "What are you looking for, young lady?" Christine hugged her and said, "Mom, I've come to give you my forgiveness."

After a moment of hesitation and surprise, the mother answered, "I was expecting you!"[12]

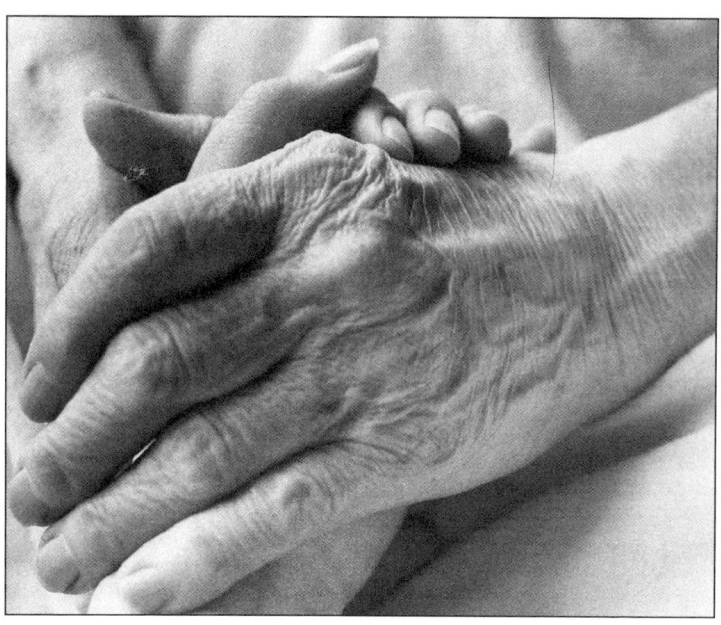

For Reflection

What do you think of the many men and women who do not rest until they discover their roots? Do you think it's only curiosity or the call of some bond that the months of pregnancy wove between mother and child?

For Christine, as for others who share the same experience, what can the commandment to honor your father and mother, mean? If possible, discuss this in a group.

Let's Celebrate the Lord Our God

In you, O Lord, do I take refuge;
let me never be put to shame!
In your righteousness deliver me and rescue me;
incline your ear to me, and save me!
Be to me a rock of refuge,
a strong fortress, to save me,
for you are my rock and my fortress.
Rescue me, O God, from the hand of the wicked,
from the grasp of the unjust and cruel man.
For you, O Lord, are my hope,
my trust, O Lord, from my youth.
Upon you I have leaned from my birth;
you are he who took me from my mother's womb.
My praise is continually of you....
Do not cast me off in the time of old age;
forsake me not when my strength is spent....
With the mighty deeds of the Lord God I will come,
I will praise your righteousness, yours alone.
O God, from my youth you have taught me,
and I still proclaim your wondrous deeds.
So even to old age and gray hairs,
O God, do not forsake me,
till I proclaim your might to all the generations
  to come.

Psalm 71:1-6, 9, 16-18

Mary Is Our Mother

Mary is the Mother to whom so many Christians confide their secrets, desires and prayers.

St. Francis of Assisi prayed to her in this way:

"I greet you, holy Lady, holy Queen, Mother of God, Mary....

You in whom there was and is all fullness of grace and of every good.

I greet you, the Lord's palace, his tent.

I greet you, his dwelling place. I greet you, his garment.

I greet you, his handmaiden. I greet you, his Mother."

Mary is the one whom the Spirit of God filled with grace and many responsibilities.

Mary is the woman of the response. She was the "palace" of the Lord, but also his handmaiden, his servant, his most faithful instrument.

Looking upon Mary with love, the poet Dante called her: "Virgin Mother, daughter of your Son, most humble and exalted of all creatures, the goal determined by Eternal Counsel."

Daughter of your Son!

Only she was able to be such! Only to her did God grant this grace!

Only Mary was able to be so fully both the daughter of the Lord and his mother.

She knew the inexpressible joy of bearing the Son within her, the pain of motherhood, the indescribable suffering of seeing him die. Her Son and yet not her Son.

But she also knew the intimacy and sweetness of being a daughter. She knew the love that comes from God the Father and the respect due to human parents. At the same time, she knew the secret of feeling herself enveloped in an immense, uncontainable Fatherhood, who asked of her things never asked of another person, who brought about in her mysteries which no reason can explain.

Mary is mother and daughter, she honors father and mother; she honors the Son whom God chose to place in her home.

Mary is the mother of parents and of children.

She is the mother of all those children of life who accept life as a gift, who don't reject it, who don't consider it either useful or useless, because it is a gift.

She is the mother of those who accept their role as servants, as instruments of life, so that through them life is brought forth, and with it goodness, beauty and mercy.

To Mary, then, we parents and children can entrust our disappointments, hopes, uncertainties, doubts, failures and revivals.

A wonderful prayer from the eastern Church can help us pray to her:

O our gentle Queen, Mother of God, our hope, friend of the orphaned, advocate of pilgrims, joy of the afflicted, protector of the oppressed, look upon our misery and affliction. Help us who are powerless, nourish us pilgrims. You who know our misery, free us, because you want to do so and we have no other help outside of you, no other protection, no other comfort than you, O Mother of God. Keep and protect us, forever and ever. Amen.

Notes

1. Gibran, K. *The Prophet.* New York: Walker and company, 1986, pp. 21-22.

2. John Paul II. *The Role of the Christian Family in the Modern World (Familiaris Consortio).* Boston: Pauline Books & Media, 1981, n. 37.

3. Martini, C.M. *Ephphatha,* I, 1, b.

4. John Paul II. *Ibid.,* n. 43.

5. Bonhoeffer, D. *Letters and Papers from Prison.* New York: The Macmillan Company, 1971, pp. 42-43.

6. Boff, L. . *sacramenti della vita.* Rome: Edizioni Borla, pp. 16-17.

7. Moro, A.C. in *Famiglie a Roma* II, n. 2, p. 2.

8. Tettamanzi, d. *Eutanasia.* Casole Monferrato: Piemme, 1985, p. 16.

9. Dela Potterie, I. *Studi di Cristologia Giovannea.* Genoa: Marietti, 1986, p. 164.

10. Pesch; O.H. *I dieci comandamenti.* Brescia: Queriniana, 1978.

11. V.D. "Il problema degli anziani," in *Lampade viventi,* n. 12, 1968, p. 314.

12. Sartor, G. *Il sole sulle colline nere.* Milan: Edizioni Paoline, 1986, pp. 50-51.

About the Author

Paul Tammi was ordained a priest of the diocese of Rome in 1982. He holds degrees in Church law and moral theology, and teaches Christian ethics at the Catholic University in Rome.

About this Series

These booklets are intended to help today's young (and not-so-young) adult explore how the ten commandments and eight beatitudes relate to human life and divine realities: How and where do they fit into contemporary culture and God's plan for us? The editors hope that *Reflections on the Commandments* will stimulate both deeper reflection and further research.

Booklets in this series: I Am the Lord Your God; You Shall Not Have Strange Gods Before Me; You Shall Not Take the Lord's Name in Vain; Remember to Keep Holy the Lord's Day; Honor Your Father and Your Mother; You Shall Not Kill; You Shall Not Commit Adultery, Nor Covet Your Neighbor's Wife; You Shall Not Steal, Nor Covet Your Neighbor's Goods; You Shall Not Bear False Witness; Blessed Are the Poor in Spirit.

St. Paul Book & Media Centers

ALASKA
  750 West 5th Ave., Anchorage, AK 99501; 907-272-8183

CALIFORNIA
  3908 Sepulveda Blvd., Culver City, CA 90230; 310-397-8676
  5945 Balboa Ave., San Diego, CA 92111; 619-565-9181
  46 Geary Street, San Francisco, CA 94108; 415-781-5180

FLORIDA
  145 S.W. 107th Ave., Miami, FL 33174; 305-559-6715

HAWAII
  1143 Bishop Street, Honolulu, HI 96813; 808-521-2731

ILLINOIS
  172 North Michigan Ave., Chicago, IL 60601; 312-346-4228

LOUISIANA
  4403 Veterans Memorial Blvd., Metairie, LA 70006; 504-887-7631

MASSACHUSETTS
  50 St. Paul's Ave., Jamaica Plain, Boston, MA 02130; 617-522-8911
  Rte. 1, 885 Providence Hwy., Dedham, MA 02026; 617-326-5385

MISSOURI
  9804 Watson Rd., St. Louis, MO 63126; 314-965-3512

NEW JERSEY
  561 U.S. Route 1, Wick Plaza, Edison, NJ 08817; 908-572-1200

NEW YORK
  150 East 52nd Street, New York, NY 10022; 212-754-1110
  78 Fort Place, Staten Island, NY 10301; 718-447-5071

OHIO
  2105 Ontario Street, Cleveland, OH 44115; 216-621-9427

PENNSYLVANIA
  510 Holstein Street, Bridgeport, PA 19405; 610-277-7728

SOUTH CAROLINA
  243 King Street, Charleston, SC 29401; 803-577-0175

TENNESSEE
  4811 Poplar Ave., Memphis, TN 38117; 901-761-2987

TEXAS
  114 Main Plaza, San Antonio, TX 78205; 210-224-8101

VIRGINIA
  1025 King Street, Alexandria, VA 22314; 703-549-3806

GUAM
  285 Farenholt Ave., Suite 308, Tamuning, Guam 96911; 671-649-4377

CANADA
  3022 Dufferin Street, Toronto, Ontario, Canada M6B 3T5; 416-781-9131